SUPER STRUCTURES OF THE WORLD

THE SEAWOLF SUBMARINE

BLACKBIRCH®
PRESS

THOMSON
✴
GALE

San Diego • Detroit • New York • San Francisco • Cleveland • New Haven, Conn. • Waterville, Maine • London • Munich

THOMSON

✦

GALE

Photo credits: cover, pages all © Discovery Communications, Inc. except for pages 3, 29, 44 ©
Blackbirch Press Archives; pages 9, 10, 15, 22-23, 24-25, 32-33, 36-37 © CORBIS. Image on bottom banner © PhotoDisc

LIBRARY OF CONGRESS CATALOGING–IN–PUBLICATION DATA

Seawolf submarine / Elaine Pascoe, book editor.
    p. cm. — (Super structures of the world)
Summary: Examines the history of the most advanced nuclear submarine ever built, the
Seawolf, including some of the challenges faced in design and construction amid of
post-Cold War budget constraints.
Includes bibliographical references and index.
  ISBN 1-56711-868-2 (hardback : alk. paper) — ISBN 1-4103-0188-5 (pbk. : alk. paper)
  1. Seawolf (Submarine)—Juvenile literature. [1. Seawolf (Submarine)
2. Submarines (Ships)—Design and construction.] I. Pascoe, Elaine. II. Series.

VA65.S43 2004
623.8'2574—dc22   2003007518

Printed in China
10 9 8 7 6 5 4 3 2 1

THE SEAWOLF

Rising from beneath the waves, a silent predator suddenly strikes....
   For almost a century, submarines have patrolled the world's oceans.
Their missions, even their construction, have been cloaked in secrecy.
This is the inside story of the most advanced nuclear submarine ever
built, perhaps the most complex military machine of the twentieth
century—a super structure called *Seawolf*. Launched in 1996, *Seawolf*
took its place in the ocean as the most advanced and lethal submarine
ever created.

Above: Seawolf is the deadliest and most advanced nuclear submarine.

The USS *Seawolf* was designed to be a ship for the next century, the first of an entirely new class of submarines. It took more than three thousand workers more than a decade to build the sub. The crew endured years of training to earn a place aboard this mechanical marvel.

Top and Middle: More than three thousand people worked to build the sophisticated submarine. Bottom: The navy submarine program worked for more than a decade to bring Seawolf *to life.*

When the 14 officers and 124 enlisted men began their first mission—a complex and dangerous series of tests known as sea trials—they and the submarine's builder were under intense scrutiny. In the defense–budget cutbacks that followed the Cold War, the number of Seawolf-class submarines approved for construction was slashed from thirty to three. If this ship failed her sea trials, the entire future of the U.S. Navy submarine program could be affected. That would be a blow not only to the service, but also to the men and women who design and build these amazing machines.

Above: Naval officers and enlisted men participated in a series of sea trials in a mission to prove Seawolf worthy. Left: Following budget cuts, only three submarines were approved for the first Seawolf class.

A NEW DESIGN

While the construction of *Seawolf* was a new chapter in the history of underwater vehicles, its life began on the design table. When *Seawolf* was designed in the 1980s, the computer revolution was just beginning. With the advent of computer assisted design, or CAD technology, her creators could drastically reduce the staggering amount of hand calculations required. Now, basic design measurements, such as length and diameter, could be visualized in ways the early pioneers of submarines couldn't imagine. But the design process was still full of challenges.

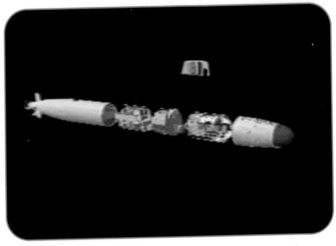

Top: **Seawolf** *was originally designed in the 1980s, at the start of a new technology age. Bottom: The computer revolution allowed high-tech programs to assist in the creation of the submarine.*

The three main problems facing modern navy designers were also faced by their forefathers: how to create a vehicle that could stay underwater for extended periods of time, how to install enough weaponry to make it a viable threat, and how to remain undetected. In the past, submarines were constructed by welding together steel plates to form the hull. Then the machinery, or guts, of the sub would be lowered inside through openings in the top. This was the primary method of submarine construction from World War I through the Cold War.

Above: Builders struggled to make a submarine that would be undetectable on radar.

Right: Designers used computer programs to determine how Seawolf would stay underwater for long stretches of time.

The Cold War was one of the most volatile and dangerous times in American history. As the arms race between the United States and the Soviet Union escalated, the government turned to its undersea force for defense. The U.S. Navy developed two submarine classes, the ballistic missile submarine and the attack class. The ballistic subs, often called boomers because of their enormous firepower, were essentially large mobile platforms for launching nuclear weapons. Deployed on secret missions throughout the world's oceans, the ballistic missile submarines served as a threatening deterrent to an enemy first strike. Their companion class, the attack subs, were smaller and faster. These subs were designed to do exactly what their name implied—attack quickly, silently, and with deadly force.

Following the Cold War, the threat of a superpower conflict decreased, while the likelihood of smaller, regional conflicts increased. In response, a new kind of submarine was needed, a submarine like *Seawolf*.

Left: During the Cold War, the U.S. Navy created two submarine classes prior to Seawolf. The ballistic subs launched nuclear weapons and the attack subs were lethal weapons.

For this new class of submarine, a new building approach was employed. For the first time, a submarine was built as a series of modules, with the piping, machinery, and fittings installed at the same time. This new method of construction made maintenance much easier. In the past, engineers had to cut holes in the hull to add or remove machinery. Now machinery can fit through special openings that are covered by a watertight hatch. Modular construction also results in a stronger hull. As it slips beneath the waves, the hull of a submarine must withstand bone-crushing pressures. Even a pencil-sized puncture in the ship's hull would bring in water with the velocity of a bullet fired from a rifle.

This page: The hull is one of the strongest parts of the submarine and sustains the most pressure.

Left: Submarine graves were common during World War II, when thousands of Americans died under Japanese attack.

Submariners are well aware of the dangers. During World War II, submarine crews in the Pacific faced impossible odds with terrifying regularity. Under constant attack from Japanese depth charges, submarines became the final resting places for thousands of American servicemen.

Despite the losses, American submarines inflicted major damage on the Japanese navy and merchant fleet. One after the other, these steel sharks rolled out of shipyards as fast as they could be built. The American submarine fleet dramatically affected the war's outcome. Although submarines represented just 2 percent of the navy, they accounted for 55 percent of all the Japanese ship sinkings in the war.

Right: The view through the periscope of a submarine

SUBS GO NUCLEAR

Ultimately, the end of World War II was brought on by a catastrophic new weapon, the atomic bomb. After the war's end, one man began experimenting with a way to safely harness the enormous power of nuclear energy to build a new kind of submarine, one with incomparable speed and stealth. His vision would lead to the awesome creation called *Seawolf*. As *Seawolf* cuts silent-ly through the water, its nuclear reactor supplies an almost limitless amount of energy. Four pounds of enriched uranium will provide the same amount of energy as 10 million gallons of the fuel oil used by early diesel-powered subs.

Above: The explosion of the atomic bomb over Japan jumpstarted the nuclear age.

Left: As the concept of nuclear weapons moved to the forefront during the Cold War, the vision of Seawolf was born.

Left: Navy admiral Hyman Rickover linked the submarine with the concept of nuclear power, effectively removing the need for resurfacing—the craft's vulnerable quality.

The advent of nuclear power was the most important development in the history of submarine construction. It was the dream of one man, Navy admiral Hyman Rickover. A qualified submariner and engineer, Admiral Rickover was the first person to realize that nuclear power could turn the submarine into the most feared weapon on the planet. With this new power source, Rickover reasoned, he could counteract the submarine's Achilles' heel: the need for frequent resurfacing, which made it vulnerable to attack. Nuclear propulsion turned submarines from surface ships that were capable of submerging once in a while to true submersible craft.

Harnessing the power of the atom to power a submarine was a complex problem. But once accomplished, using that power to propel the sub was relatively simple.

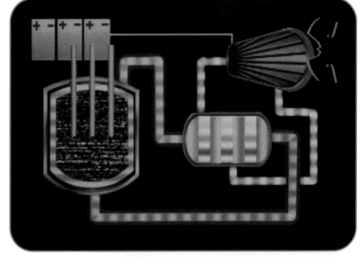

The process begins with a controlled nuclear reaction that produces extraordinary heat. Liquid pumped through the system carries that heat away from the reactor core. The heated liquid then flows through a heat exchanger, where the high temperatures turn water coursing through thick pipes into saturated steam. The steam powers a turbine, which drives a generator supplying all

the electrical energy needed to operate the ship. Excess power is stored in massive banks of batteries on board. There is no release of radioactive materials during the energy exchange process.

Top: Rickover's idea was to use nuclear power to propel the submarine.
Bottom: Nuclear reaction is used to develop heat through saturated steam.
The excess power is stored on board.

This page: Nuclear propulsion allows submarines to become true submersible crafts.

Admiral Rickover understood that nuclear engines could not only generate more power, but could also give submarines virtually unlimited range. In 1955, his theory was put to the test as USS *Nautilus* became the world's first nuclear-powered submarine—and the fastest of its day.

Above: Rickover recognized that nuclear engines would generate more power and give the submarines unlimited range.

Right: The idea of unlimited range was successfully tested in 1955 with the first nuclear-powered submarine.

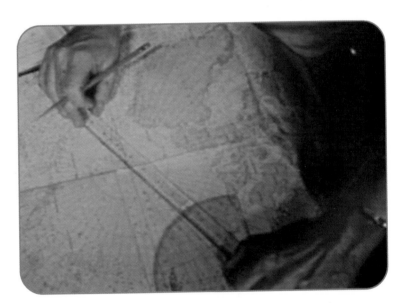

Three years later, *Nautilus* proved the submarine was now master of all the oceans, even those that were largely unexplored. In a historic four-day journey, *Nautilus* crossed from the Pacific to the Atlantic under the ice packs of the North Pole, completing the first undersea transit of this hostile environment. The same year, a different atomic submarine established a new endurance record for underwater operation. For sixty days, from August 7 to October 6, 1958, this ship remained submerged beneath the forbidding ice floes of the North Pole. The name of that ship was USS *Seawolf*, predecessor to today's nuclear-powered wonder.

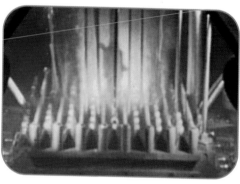

Top: Nuclear power allowed the submarine to stay underwater for sixty days, a record in 1958. Middle and bottom: The USS Seawolf is an advanced machine that uses nuclear technology.

ONBOARD TODAY'S *SEAWOLF*

For today's *Seawolf*, submerging for sixty days is simply routine. With its nuclear-powered engines and ability to manufacture oxygen and water, *Seawolf* could theoretically remain underwater for years at a time. But beyond her extended range, nuclear power has also given *Seawolf* another important edge—speed.

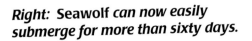

Right: Seawolf *can now easily submerge for more than sixty days.*

Left: Officers can run Seawolf *underwater for years at a time.*

While her top speed is a closely guarded navy secret, officials admit she cruises faster than twenty-five knots, about thirty miles per hour. Experts privately acknowledge *Seawolf* can actually travel much faster. *Seawolf* commander Dave McCall says, "People always ask the crew how fast the ship goes, and the crew will say, 'It goes so fantastically fast that stuff falls off.' It is certainly a sports car compared to the other ones." In fact, even the designers of this undersea sports car were surprised by how fast she really is.

Below: The submarine's crew calls Seawolf *an "undersea sports car."*

Above: Despite all the nuclear power stored on board, no radioactive materials are released on Seawolf.

For all its hi-tech power, *Seawolf* is still a warship. And life aboard this ship is no pleasure cruise. Every square inch of *Seawolf* is designed for maximum efficiency, which does not leave much room for human comforts. The crew eats in shifts, and they've learned to live without the luxuries of space and privacy.

Left: Crew members must live in cramped space aboard Seawolf.

Below: The crew on Seawolf *eats in shifts.*

Top: Every inch of space is used efficiently on the warship.

Even the sleeping quarters are designed to save space. There are just two bunks, or racks, for every three crew members—because one of three is always on watch. The system is called "hot racking" because crew members coming off watch find racks still warm from those who just left. Some sailors actually sleep in the torpedo cradles, luxurious accommodations for taller men frustrated by confined bunks.

Top: Sleeping quarters are two bunks for every three crew members, as one person is always on watch.

Bottom: The bunk system aboard **Seawolf** *is called "hot racking."*

Seawolf designers were able to use new technologies to increase available space. For example, CD-ROM technology meant thousands of technical manuals and drawings required on early subs could be replaced by compact discs. This freed up 350 cubic feet of space and eliminated more than six tons of paper on board.

A major tactical advantage of Seawolf is her arsenal of computers, the most ever used on a naval vessel. Her communications software alone uses 6 million lines of programming code. The computer-driven sensor systems on Seawolf are so advanced, they can even pick up the most minute natural sounds of the deep-shrimp feeding in the cold waters of the Atlantic, for example. More important, Seawolf sensors can detect and identify even the quietest ships by their sound signatures. The sensors, combined with improved and highly capable heavyweight torpedoes, give the sub the capability to attack both submarines and surface ships almost at will.

Right: Seawolf's sensors are advanced enough to pick up the sounds of dolphins.

Left: Seawolf *has the ability to attack both submarines and surface ships.*

Right: High-tech devices like the CD-ROM enabled Seawolf *to remove more than six tons of paperwork.*

Left: The sensor system is run by computer programs that can identify the sound signatures of other ships.

23

THE *THRESHER* DISASTER

Crew members say comparing *Seawolf* to a nonnuclear submarine is like comparing a biplane to a jet. But for all its space-age capabilities, the job of traveling beneath the sea remains extremely dangerous. And no mission is more dangerous than the Alpha Trial, the submarine's first meeting with the sea. As the crew of USS *Seawolf* began their shakedown voyage, a mission from decades earlier casts an ominous shadow.

Top: Crew members for the Alpha Trial take the submarine out to sea for the very first time.

Middle: An American flag is raised to half-mast to honor the USS Thresher.

Bottom: The dangers of underwater travel are still prevalent today.

When USS *Thresher* was launched in July 1960 she was the first of her kind, a new class of submarine. Like *Seawolf, Thresher* faced a regular series of tests designed to further submarine exploration. But on April 10, 1963, the incredible danger associated with any undersea journey became all too clear.

Right: In 1963, Thresher, *with a crew of 129 men, broke up in the depths of the Atlantic Ocean.*

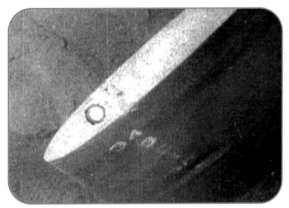

Above: Reasons for the loss of Thresher are still unknown.

At 7:47 P.M., about two hundred miles east of Boston, *Thresher* began a deep descent known as a test dive. For reasons still unknown, at 9:13 P.M., the ship radioed that it was experiencing minor difficulties and was attempting to blow its ballast tanks, a procedure used to surface during an emergency. Four minutes later a garbled message was received, then the horrifying sound of the ship breaking up. USS Thresher, along with her crew of 129 men, was gone.

Left: Navy vessels searched for remains of Thresher. The sub was finally found more than 8,000 feet below the surface.

Navy submersibles found what was left of *Thresher* in June 1963, at a depth of more than eight thousand feet. A navy court of inquiry, however, was never able to fully determine the exact cause of her demise.

No navy official was more devastated by the loss of *Thresher* than the father of nuclear submarines, Admiral Rickover. While some critics attacked the

performance of the ship's nuclear reactor, Rickover believed that submarine construction itself had to change. He lobbied for improved fabrication techniques, better inspection methods, and more attention to emerging technologies and new ways of thinking. The loss of *Thresher* forced engineers to focus on how to make submarines safer for the people who work in the harsh deep-sea environment.

Above left: Submarine construction began to change after the **Thresher** *disaster.*
Above right: More attention has been given to the safety and inspection of submarines.

DEALING WITH DANGER

The designers and builders of *Seawolf* took full advantage of new technologies. Even the body of the sub was made from a new material. The hulls of early subs were made from a high-strength steel called HY-80. This material could withstand pressure of eighty thousand pounds per square inch. The Seawolf-class submarines use a new super steel called HY-100, able to withstand one hundred thousand pounds of pressure per square inch. This material allows designers to create submarines that dive deeper than their predecessors of the same weight, although just how deep is classified. Or they can create lighter subs that are capable of reaching the same depths as the earlier, heavier subs.

Above: New technology allows lighter submarines to go to greater depths.

Above: Seawolf *builders use HY-100 super steel in the creation of the hull of the submarine.*

This page: The newer steel can withstand one hundred thousand pounds of pressure per square inch.

But regardless of its weight, a submarine's effectiveness has always been judged by its ability to remain undetected. Once at sea, an engine hum, a mechanical noise, even a crew member's conversation could reveal the ship's location, with deadly consequences.

"Stealth is the most important thing," says Navy rear admiral Robert Frick. "A submarine maintains its capability and its safety by never being detected." As long as it's undetected, a sub can conduct surveillance, monitor shipping lanes, detect and deploy mines, and conduct other missions. Just knowing that the United States has powerful submarines that can move almost anywhere quickly and in stealth may be enough to deter enemies from taking action.

Above: Navy rear admiral Robert Frick acknowledges that stealth is of the essence in successfully completing a submarine mission. Right: An undetected submarine can conduct surveillance, detect mines, and complete missions.

To maintain stealth, every joint and substructure within *Seawolf* is designed to minimize sound and vibration. Even operating at top speed, the ship is quieter than the older submarines were when idling at the pier. The ship's inner decks are not attached directly to the hull, but rest on rubber mountings to reduce vibrations. Propellers are designed to produce minimal noise. Antidetection tiles, made from sound-absorbing plastic compounds, line the inside of the hull, and an

additional layer of sound-absorbing material was applied to the hull's exterior.

While the ship is cloaked by a silent defense, sometimes the most deadly threat to a submarine crew comes from inside the ship. Says *Seawolf* commander Dave McCall, "I think fire is probably the worst thing to have happen because if you don't do the right thing it can quickly get out of control. We're in an enclosed environment, and there's nowhere else to go."

Above: Because of the sub's enclosed environment, the most deadly threat to a **Seawolf** *crew is fire.*

Trapped hundreds of feet below the ocean's surface, a fire could wipe out a crew in an instant, or slowly consume the ship's life-giving oxygen supplies. It is a terrifying scenario, but one that is planned for in the design of a ship, in its construction, and in training at the Naval Submarine School in Groton, Connecticut. Trainee submariners know that someday they may face a situation of life and death, an emergency in which their response will either save the ship or send it to the bottom of the sea.

Above: Crew members train to handle horrific circumstances while on board the submarine.

Below: Quick and accurate response in a submarine emergency can save both the vessel and crew in a situation like a fire.

This training doesn't end once on board. Submarine crews constantly rehearse and plan for every conceivable situation, from a fire in the galley to combat. Like an aircraft carrier, a submarine is divided into separate watertight sections. That way, if a torpedo should penetrate the hull, or if a fire should start in one section, the rest of the ship is still able to function.

Right: Submarine crews also train on board for various combat situations.

Left: Seawolf is divided into sections, so if disaster strikes one area, the rest of the sub can still function.

BUILDING A SUPER STRUCTURE

There are few places in the world large enough and sophisticated enough to build a nuclear submarine. The Electric Boat Company's machine shop in Quonset Point, Rhode Island, is one of them. Here, giant pipes were twisted into intricate shapes, while massive grinding machines polished tons of special metal alloys into some of the 8 million parts that became the body of *Seawolf*.

Below: The premises of a boat company in Rhode Island was the ideal place to build the nuclear-powered Seawolf.

Left: Large pipes are twisted and maneuvered to make the body of the submarine.

Once the pieces of this new nuclear submarine were forged, workers faced an imposing task—transporting the giant sections to their dry-dock facilities in Groton, Connecticut. Modules weighing more than seven hundred tons each were placed on the largest transport truck in the world and traveled by truck and barge to the Connecticut dry-dock facility. There they were suspended in order and pieced together to form the complete ship.

Top: Trucks and barges carried the heavy loads. Some modules weighed more than seven hundred tons. Above left: Transportation of the separate parts of the submarine was a difficult task. Above right: The largest transport truck in the world hauled the parts to Connecticut.

Then, with the body almost complete, the sub's weapons systems were installed. On board *Seawolf*, four levels of robotically controlled storage racks can deploy a lethal force on a moment's notice. Tomahawk cruise missiles can be placed with pinpoint accuracy, guided by a global positioning satellite. *Seawolf*'s antisubmarine missiles make her a fearsome underwater force as well.

Seawolf is the most sophisticated military craft ever created, but the road leading to this super structure actually began hundreds of years ago. It was a road paved with danger.

36

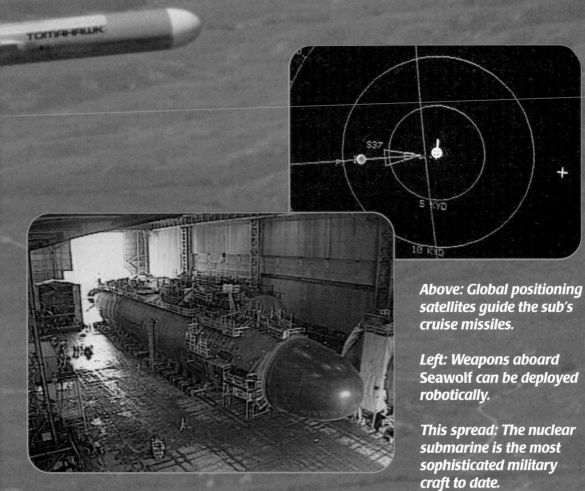

TOMAHAWK

S37

5 KYD

10 KYD

Above: Global positioning satellites guide the sub's cruise missiles.

Left: Weapons aboard Seawolf can be deployed robotically.

This spread: The nuclear submarine is the most sophisticated military craft to date.

UNDERWATER PIONEERS

In 1775, only twenty-five miles from the site of the Electric Boat Company, a young Irishman named David Bushnell built a device called the Turtle. Driven by his intense hatred of the British, and with the support of George Washington, Bushnell created an underwater craft that could place an explosive device on harbored British warships. Its name came from the design, resembling two turtle shells seven feet long and four feet wide. This craft of wood, iron, and leather could approach an enemy ship with a hand-cranked propeller and was able to stay submerged twenty feet below the surface for almost thirty minutes.

Above: In 1775, David Bushnell built the Turtle. This early submarine could stay below the ocean's surface for nearly half an hour.

Unfortunately, when Bushnell's device was tried on a British man-of-war, the attaching screw could not penetrate the copper sheathing on the warship's hull. The Turtle was lucky to escape. Still, the theory of the underwater sneak attack was born.

Bushnell's theory of the underwater sneak attack was born of these sketches, which depict the design and concept of the Turtle's sneak attack.

During the Civil War, both sides developed submarines. But it was a Confederate version invented by Horace L. Hunley that became the first sub to record a torpedo hit on an enemy ship. It was a milestone that came with a terrible cost. The sixty foot *H.L. Hunley* used a crew of

eight to turn its propeller crankshaft. In 1864, the *Hunley* towed a single torpedo into the harbor of Charleston, South Carolina, and delivered its deadly cargo against the Union's USS *Housatonic*. The attack did

little damage to the Union ship, but the exploding torpedo sank the *Hunley*.

*Above: Used during the Civil War, the **H.L. Hunley** was the first craft to send a torpedo hit on an enemy ship.*

*Left: The attack backfired on the **Hunley** when the torpedo exploded and sank the submarine.*

As primitive as those early craft were, they used the same engineering principle as today's modern subs—the ability to submerge and surface by adding or subtracting ballast. Inside the hull of a sub are ballast tanks designed to temporarily fill with water. When the tanks fill with water, the vessel sinks. When compressed air flushes the water from the compartments, buoyancy returns and the ship rises.

Above: Civil War-era submarines submerged and surfaced by adjusting the ballast.

Right: Early submarines were similar to today's crafts. They are both based on the same concept of different amounts of ballast.

Seawolf also employs this basic principle of physics. But while early sub designs placed the ballast tanks port and starboard, *Seawolf*'s tanks are located fore and aft, so the ship can submerge or surface with incredible speed.

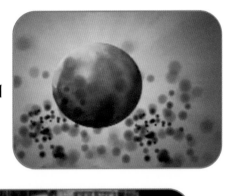

The propulsion of early subs required exhaustive manual labor, performed in suffocating spaces with no fresh air. These ships could dive only for brief periods, staying close to the surface in order to ventilate the craft. On board *Seawolf* the same nuclear power that propels the ship also supplies the

crew with life-giving oxygen. Water molecules are formed from two hydrogen atoms and a single oxygen atom. On *Seawolf*, sophisticated machines use electromagnetic force to disengage the hydrogen atoms from the molecular structure, leaving pure oxygen for the ship's life support system.

Top: Seawolf *uses water molecules to supply the sub with pure oxygen.*

Above: Early submarines could not dive for long because of ventilation restrictions.

But it was another source of energy that first turned the submarine into a viable fighting machine. John Philip Holland was an industrious Irish immigrant who pioneered a double propulsion system for submarines and cofounded the Electric Boat Company. Holland's boat used a fifty horsepower gas engine for surface sailing and, to keep the air breathable, a battery-operated motor while submerged. This dual engine approach gave the sub greater range and submergence capability, something the U.S. Navy officials realized in 1900. Able to dive to just over one hundred feet, the Irishman's craft became the first submarine commissioned by the navy. The crew of USS *Holland* became pioneers of a new world under the sea.

Below: John Philip Holland created a double–propulsion system for submarines, which allowed for greater range and submergence.

Over the next fourteen years, twenty-five more of these amazing devices called submarines were built. But beneath the waves, the United States would not be alone for long. In May 1915, the ocean liner *Lusitania* was fired upon and sunk by a German U-boat. In less than twenty minutes, more than 1,100 passengers died, many of them Americans. The United States moved one step closer to war with Germany.

During World War I, the potential of the new machine would be put to the ultimate test. The age-old ritual of enemies facing each other in head-to-head combat was replaced by the sneak attack. The submarine forever changed the nature of warfare.

Opposite page: The U.S. Navy built several more submarines in the early 1900s, including this World War II vessel.

Below left: In 1915, a German U-boat attack on the Lusitania *killed more than 1,100 people.*

Below right: Submarine warfare became the new combat technique during World War I.

CLEAN SWEEP

When *Seawolf* returned to her base at Groton, Connecticut, at the end of her maiden voyage, a simple wooden broom attached to the ship's superstructure told observers everything they needed to know. The ship had performed a clean sweep of her first major test. Her propulsion and life support systems had been put through their paces. She had performed rapid dives to classified depths. Under stressful warfare scenarios, she had been deemed combat ready.

Against a backdrop of budget cuts and shifting political power structures, the designers, builders, and crew of USS *Seawolf* achieved a stunning victory. Under a mandate to do more with less, they rewrote the book on how to build a submarine. The success of *Seawolf* will provide a blueprint for the next class of attack submarines, and for a new generation of submariners who will pilot these guardians of the deep into the future.

Above: **Seawolf** *has opened the doors for future submarine designs with its success in the depths of the ocean.*

GLOSSARY

aft the back of a ship or aircraft

ballast weights in the hold of a ship that enhance stability; in a submarine, water is used

buoyancy the tendency of a body to float when put underwater

cAD computer-aided design

classified withheld from the public for the reason of national security

cruise missile a missile guided by a terrain-following radar system

depth charge a drum filled with explosives used to attack submarines

fore the front of a ship or aircraft

hot racking the practice of having three sailors rotate on two sleeping bunks on a submarine

mine an explosive placed underwater or underground that detonates if disturbed

nuclear reaction a process that alters the energy or structure of atomic nuclei

port the left side of a ship or aircraft

propulsion forward movement

starboard the right side of a ship or aircraft

stealth proceeding secretly or unseen

surveillance close watch kept over something or someone

turbine a rotary engine that is turned by rushing water

uranium a metal element used to generate nuclear power

INDEX